Celebrate

COLORING BOOK

Alexandra Cowell

DOVER PUBLICATIONS, INC.
MINEOLA, NEW YORK

Bibliographical Note

Celebrate Coloring Book: Your Passport to Calm is a new work, first published by
Dover Publications, Inc., in 2017.

International Standard Book Number
ISBN-13: 978-0-486-81382-0
ISBN-10: 0-486-81382-7

Manufactured in China by RR Donnelley
81382701   2017
www.doverpublications.com

bliss

\\'blis\\

noun

1. supreme happiness; utter joy or contentment

2. heaven; paradise

3. your passport to calm

Take a pleasant journey into a world of relaxation with *BLISS Celebrate Coloring Book: Your Passport to Calm*. Bring to life a variety of happy occasions by adding color to 46 different designs featuring weddings, anniversaries, graduations, birthdays, special holidays, and other celebratory events. Now you can travel to your newly found retreat of peace and serenity whenever you'd like with this petite-sized collection of sophisticated artwork.

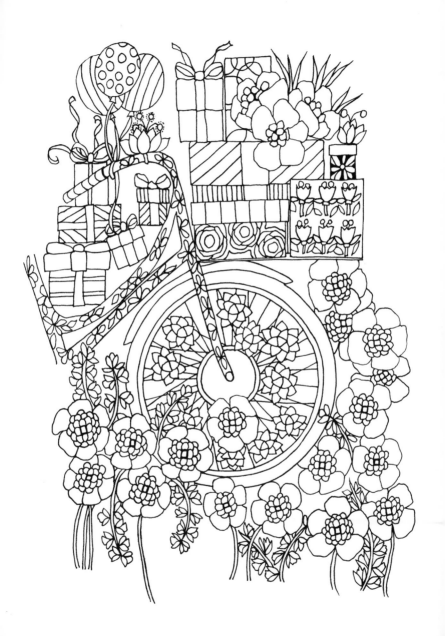

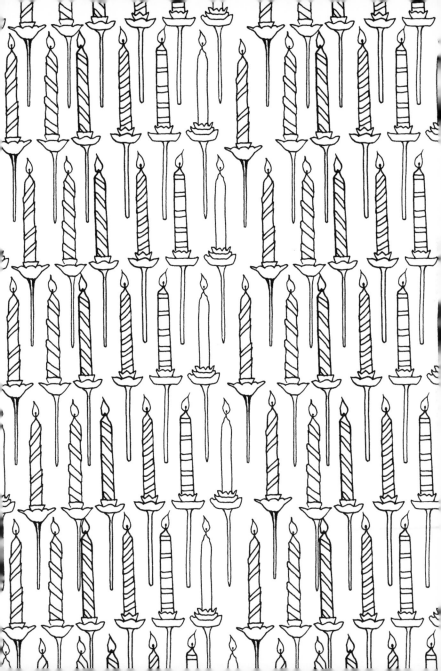

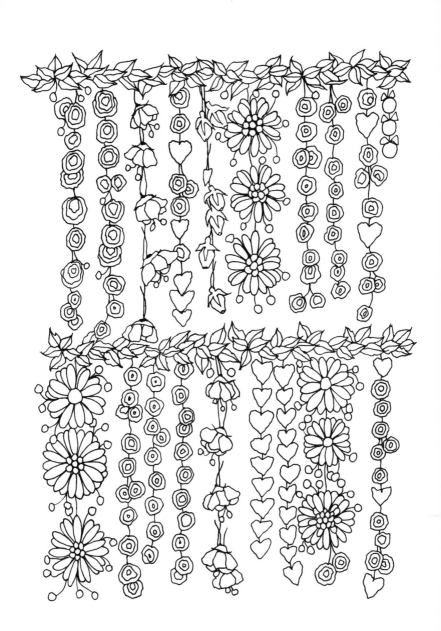

Party Dress